LIVING IN THE WILD: SEA MAMMALS

SEALS

Claire Throp

Raintree is an imprint of Capstone Global Library Limited, a company incorporated in England and Wales having its registered office at 7 Pilgrim Street, London, EC4V 6LB – Registered company number: 6695582

www.raintreepublishers.co.uk
myorders@raintreepublishers.co.uk

Edited by Adam Miller, Andrew Farrow, and Laura Knowles
Designed by Steve Mead
Picture research by Mica Brančić
Original illustrations © Capstone Global Library Ltd 2013
Illustrations by HL Studios
Originated by Capstone Global Library Ltd
Printed and bound in China by CTPS

ISBN 978 1 406 25011 4 (hardback)
16 15 14 13 12
10 9 8 7 6 5 4 3 2 1

ISBN 978 1 406 25018 3 (paperback)
17 16 15 14
10 9 8 7 6 5 4 3 2 1

British Library Cataloguing in Publication Data
Throp, Claire.
Seals. -- (Living in the wild. Sea animals)
599.7'9-dc23
A full catalogue record for this book is available from the British Library.

Acknowledgements
We would like to thank the following for permission to reproduce photographs: Alamy pp. 13 (© JTB Photo Communications, Inc.), 24 (© WILDLIFE GmbH), 25 (© Images & Stories), 26 (© Danita Delimont), 27 (© Cody Duncan), 32 (© WorldFoto), 44 (© Clemente do Rosario); Corbis pp. 7 (© Paul Souders), 15 (© DLILLC), 22 (Minden Pictures/ © Flip Nicklin), 33 (Ecoscene/© Graham Neden), 38 (epa/ © Adam Warawa); FLPA pp. 9 (Minden Pictures/Yva Momatiuk & John Eastcott), 17 (Minden Pictures/Flip Nicklin); Nature Picture Library pp. 10 (© Doug Perrine), 30 (© Doug Allan), 31 (© Ingo Arndt), 35 (© ARCO), 37 (© Alex Mustard), 39 (© Alex Mustard); Photoshot pp. 14 (© Tetra Images), 18 (© NHPA/Michael Patrick O'Neill), 23 (© NHPA/David Tipling), 28 (© NHPA/Ernie Janes), 36 (© WpNPhoto/HSUS/ Brian Skerry), 41 (© NHPA/Kevin Schafer), Shutterstock pp. 4 (© FloridaStock), 16 (© wcpmedia), 19 (© Lee Torrens), 29 (© Wild Arctic Pictures), 42 (© worldswildlifewonders).

Cover photograph of an elephant seal reproduced with permission of Shutterstock/ © Olon7.

Every effort has been made to contact copyright holders of any material reproduced in this book. Any omissions will be rectified in subsequent printings if notice is given to the publisher.

Disclaimer
All the internet addresses (URLs) given in this book were valid at the time of going to press. However, due to the dynamic nature of the internet, some addresses may have changed, or sites may have changed or ceased to exist since publication. While the author and publisher regret any inconvenience this may cause readers, no responsibility for any such changes can be accepted by either the author or the publisher.

Contents

Some words are shown in bold, **like this**. You can find out what they mean by looking in the glossary.

What are sea mammals?

What's that deafening noise? A group of Antarctic fur seals resting on the beach are suddenly disturbed. Two huge male seals are fighting over the right to mate. It's an amazing sight!

Seals and sea lions are sea **mammals**. Mammals have a backbone, fur or hair on their body, and use lungs to breathe. They give birth to live young and mothers feed their babies milk. Does this description sound familiar? It should – humans are also mammals.

Harp seals are born on the ice and the young seals are famous for their white fur. Harp seals can live up to the age of 35 and can be found from Newfoundland in Canada to northern Russia.

Sea mammals live and feed in the sea. Different types of sea mammal include: whales and dolphins; seals, sea lions, and walruses; manatees and dugongs; sea otters; and polar bears.

Common features

Seals, sea lions, and walruses have large flippers that are useful for swimming but some types can use their flippers to move on land, too. Most have to come onto land or ice to mate, give birth, **suckle** their young, and **moult**. They spend most of their life at sea and have thick layers of **blubber** to help them cope with the cold water.

HOW OLD?

It is possible to find out the age of a sea lion by counting the growth rings in its teeth, much like people do with tree growth rings. When a sea lion dies, a slice of one of its teeth can be taken. Scientists colour the tooth so that the growth rings show up and can be counted.

Meet the sea mammals

There are around 130 different types, or **species**, of sea mammal. They have adapted in different ways to live in the sea:

Type of sea mammal	How do they move?	Where do they live?
Whales and dolphins	use tail, fins, and flippers	These sea mammals live in water all the time.
Manatees and dugongs	use tail and flippers	
Seals, sea lions, and walruses	use flippers	These sea mammals spend some of their time in water, and some on land.
Sea otters	use legs and tail	
Polar bears	use legs	

What are seals?

There are two families of seals: eared seals (Otariidae), including sea lions, and true or earless seals (Phocidae). The diagram below shows the main differences between them. The most obvious difference is that eared seals have external ears that are visible on the sides of their head. True seals do have ears, but they are hidden. There is also a difference in the size and use of flippers.

Seals spend most of their life in water so all are excellent swimmers and divers. When on land, some species spend their time in groups known as colonies, in nesting sites called rookeries. Males are known as bulls, females are cows, and babies are called pups.

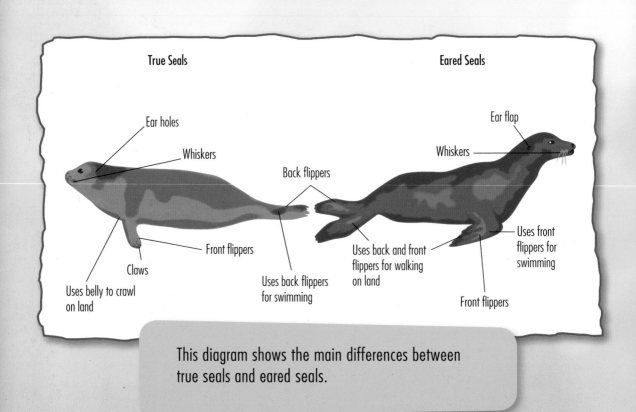

True Seals

Ear holes

Whiskers

Back flippers

Front flippers

Claws

Uses belly to crawl on land

Uses back flippers for swimming

Eared Seals

Ear flap

Whiskers

Uses back and front flippers for walking on land

Uses front flippers for swimming

Front flippers

This diagram shows the main differences between true seals and eared seals.

Size

Usually male seals are larger than females – sometimes a lot larger! The female Weddell seal, however, is bigger than the male. Seals range in size from the small Baikal seal to the huge Southern elephant seal. Baikal seals measure only 1.4 metres (4 ½ feet) long and weigh up to 70 kilograms (154 pounds). Male Southern elephant seals can grow to more than 6 metres (20 feet) long and weigh 4,000 kilograms (8,800 pounds)!

BURNEY LEBOEUF

Burney LeBoeuf of the University of California has been studying elephant seals for many years. He has researched their behaviour, feeding, and diving habits. He has even been involved in a project to discover a way of **tagging** seals to hear what they hear as they dive under water.

Whiskers are one of the most sensitive parts of a seal's body. The bearded seal is so-called because of its huge whiskers.

How are seals classified?

Classification is the way in which scientists group living things together according to the characteristics that they share. This allows us to identify living things and help us understand why they live where they do and behave the way they do.

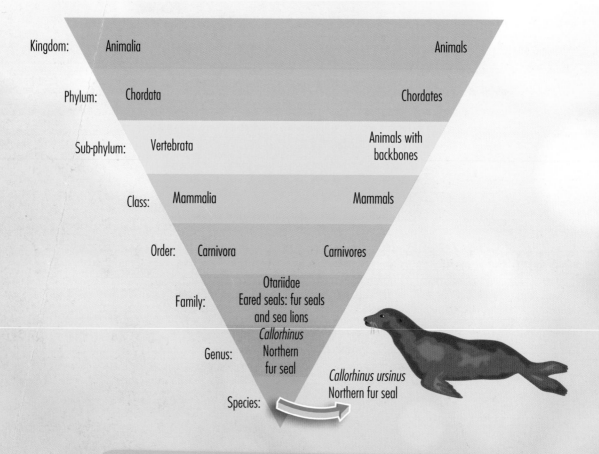

Kingdom:	Animalia	Animals
Phylum:	Chordata	Chordates
Sub-phylum:	Vertebrata	Animals with backbones
Class:	Mammalia	Mammals
Order:	Carnivora	Carnivores
Family:	Otariidae	Eared seals: fur seals and sea lions
Genus:	*Callorhinus*	Northern fur seal
Species:		*Callorhinus ursinus* Northern fur seal

This chart shows how the Northern fur seal is classified.

Classification groups

In classification, animals are split into various groups. The standard groups are Kingdom, Phylum, Class, Order, Family, Genus, and Species. Sometimes, further classification involves adding more groups such as a sub-order or infra-order. Each of the standard groups contains fewer and fewer members. For example, there are far more animals in the class Mammalia (mammals) than animals in the family Phocidae (true seals). Animals are given an internationally recognized two-part Latin name. This helps to avoid confusion if animals are known by different common names in different countries. The common or harbour seal's Latin name is *Phoca vitulina*, for example.

Eared seals

The family Otariidae, which means "little ears", includes 14 species of eared seals: nine are fur seals and six are sea lions. Apart from the Northern fur seal, seven species of fur seal live in the southern **hemisphere** and the Guadalupe fur seal lives on Mexico's Guadalupe Island. Eared seals are **social**, particularly during the **breeding** season. Eared seals can walk on land by turning their back flippers around so that they act like feet. They all have thick layers of fur and range in size from the huge Cape fur seal to the much smaller Galapagos fur seal.

Northern fur seals spend much of their life in the North Pacific Ocean.

Sea lions

Sea lions are in the same family as the fur seals – the Otariidae. Sea lions are bigger than most fur seals but their fur is not as thick. They have large front and back flippers. The largest is Steller's sea lion. Male sea lions are much bigger than females, and can reach 3 metres (10 feet) in length. Sea lions gather in large groups called rookeries. At breeding time males fight each other to mate with groups of females. The California sea lion is the best known because it is seen in marine parks around the world.

Sea lions, such as these young Galápagos sea lions, have many similar features to fur seals.

True seals

There are 18 species in the Phocidae family. A sub-family – the southern phocids – includes monk seals, elephant seals, and the Antarctic seals. Northern phocids include the bearded seal, the hooded seal, the grey seal, and a number of species related to the common or harbour seal.

True seals do not have an external ear and they have shorter front flippers than back flippers. Many true seals give birth to pups that have very soft white fur.

Some phocids are solitary, while others gather in small groups. While most true seals are awkward on land, some can move faster than humans. Crabeater seals are able to move faster on ice than a human can run.

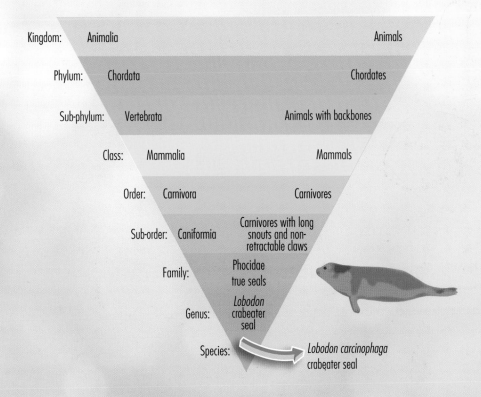

Kingdom:	Animalia	Animals
Phylum:	Chordata	Chordates
Sub-phylum:	Vertebrata	Animals with backbones
Class:	Mammalia	Mammals
Order:	Carnivora	Carnivores
Sub-order:	Caniformia	Carnivores with long snouts and non-retractable claws
Family:	Phocidae true seals	
Genus:	*Lobodon* crabeater seal	
Species:	*Lobodon carcinophaga* crabeater seal	

This chart shows how the crabeater seal is classified.

Where do seals live?

A **habitat** is the place where an animal lives. The habitat has to provide everything the animal needs from food to shelter. An animal is dependent on its habitat.

Seals live in oceans all over the world, particularly in the **polar regions**. Baikal seals are one of the few seals to only live in freshwater habitats. They mainly live in Lake Baikal in Russia. The Caspian seal is only found in the Caspian Sea on the eastern edge of Europe. When different species of seals come out of the sea, they like a range of habitats. Common seals spend time in calm bays and when they come ashore they prefer sandy beaches. California sea lions love rocky shores, while Weddell seals rest and mate on **pack ice** in the Antarctic.

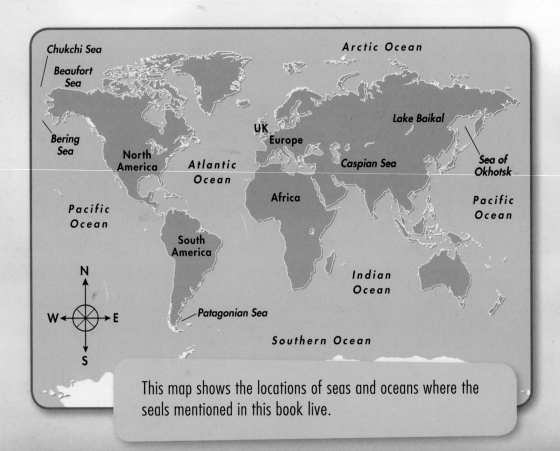

This map shows the locations of seas and oceans where the seals mentioned in this book live.

Migration

Many seal species **migrate**. Harp seals usually travel in large groups after moulting in late spring. They migrate from the North Atlantic Ocean near North America to the Arctic for the summer. Research has shown that southern elephant seals migrate more than 10,000 kilometres (6,200 miles) in search of food in a year.

EXTRA USEFUL SEAL RESEARCH

Some seals and sea lions have helped us learn more about the Patagonian Sea near South America in the Atlantic Ocean. **Transmitters** were attached to 16 different species of sea animals so that scientists could follow their movements. This research provided information that was used in the first ever atlas of the Patagonian Sea, which was published in 2009.

Ribbon seals spend their time on pack ice or in open water in the North Pacific and Bering Sea.

What adaptations help seals survive?

An **adaptation** is something that allows an animal to live in a particular place in a particular way. Animals develop adaptations as species **evolve** over thousands of years.

Body shape

A seal's body is round in the middle and tapered or pointed at both ends. It is streamlined, which means it is long and smooth. This body shape is perfect for moving through water easily. Flippers are also important for swimming. They are broad and flat and act like paddles. Eared seals use their front flippers to swim and their back flippers for steering. True seals are the opposite – they use their back flippers to swim and their front flippers for steering and for balance when swimming slowly.

Fur seals and sea lions can use their back flippers to help them walk.

Sea lions like these have nails on their back flipper to scratch any itches.

Flippers and claws

Seals and sea lions are not as graceful on land as they are in water. Eared seals, including sea lions, can turn their back flippers around and use them like feet to "walk" on land. True seals cannot do this so they shuffle along the ground.

While true seals have claws on all their flippers, sea lions and fur seals only have claws on their back flippers. These are used for scratching and cleaning their fur. The claws on the front flippers of true seals are also used for scratching and **grooming**, and are also useful for pulling themselves along while moving on land. Some seals that live in the polar regions, such as the ringed seal, use their claws for opening breathing holes in the ice.

Keeping warm

Seals and sea lions have a thick layer of body fat called blubber on their bodies. This blubber helps to keep them warm in the cold sea as heat is lost far quicker in water than in air. Blubber is also a useful supply of food for times when seals cannot hunt, for example when females are nursing their young.

Fur also helps to prevent heat loss. Oil from **glands** in a seal's body gets mixed through its fur and helps to make it waterproof, helping to keep the seal warm.

Blubber smooths out the seal's body, helping to streamline its shape.

TEETH FOR ALL FOODS

The teeth of leopard seals are adapted for the wide range of food they eat. Sharp front teeth are used to bite and hold on to larger prey. Their back teeth have big spaces in them for filtering **krill**.

Eyesight

Seals' large eyes have good vision, even under water. A Ross seal has huge eyes, measuring 60 millimetres (2.4 inches) across the widest part. A seal's pupils can also get very big to help let in as much light as possible. However, it is thought that they do not have colour vision or at the most only a range of green and blue colours. Seals and walruses have a reflecting layer of cells behind their eye called a *tapetum lucidum*. This helps them to see at night. The *tapetum* is the reason why seals' eyes can shine brightly if a photograph is taken of them under water.

Hearing and smell

Sound travels faster and further in water than it does in air. Seals have excellent hearing, particularly in water. This helps them to locate prey. Out of water, their hearing is not as good – although still as good as that of humans – but seals use it to find their pups. Mothers also use smell to recognize their pups. Seals have a good sense of smell when they are on land.

Seals and sea lions can dive to great depths for long periods of time. This Australian sea lion can dive up to 275 metres (900 feet).

Touch

Seals have sensitive whiskers called vibrissae. They are supported by very strong muscles. Seals can move each whisker on its own, but mainly they sweep their whiskers from side to side to detect vibrations in the water made by fish swimming. These sensitive whiskers help seals to find prey even in dark, murky water.

A seal's whiskers help it to sense the shape and size of its prey.

Diving

Seals close their ears and nostrils to keep water out while they dive. They also breathe out first, so they aren't affected by **water pressure**. Other adaptations help them to stay under water for longer. Seals have more blood in their bodies than land mammals, which means they can take in more oxygen before they dive. Blood moves to the heart, lungs, and brain, where it is needed the most. The seal's heart rate slows, using up less oxygen. Southern elephant seals dive the deepest: the deepest recorded was nearly 2,400 metres (7,875 feet).

What do seals eat?

Living things in any habitat depend on each other. This is called **interdependence**. Animals eat other animals or plants in order to get energy. They in turn may be eaten by bigger animals. These links between animals and plants are called **food chains**. Many connected food chains add up to make a **food web**.

A food chain starts with a plant because plants are the only **organisms** that can make their own food. They are called producers. In an ocean food web, phytoplankton, algae, and plants, such as sea grasses, are producers. Animals are consumers because they consume, or eat, other animals.

Seals are called carnivores because they eat meat. Animals that eat other animals are known as predators. The animals they eat are known as prey.

A variety of food

Seals' diet often depends on the season and where they live. They are known as opportunistic feeders because they eat such a range of food. Seals mainly eat krill, squid, crustaceans such as shrimp, and fish, such as herring or salmon. Seals either swallow small prey whole or tear off chunks of prey and then swallow the pieces without chewing.

WHY IS IT IMPORTANT TO KNOW WHAT SEALS EAT?

Many seal researchers spend time looking at scats, or seal poo! The reason is to help them find out what seals eat. Around the coast of Scotland, researchers are trying to work out why grey seals are thriving but common seals are not. Their diet may show if competition for food with grey seals is a major problem for common seals.

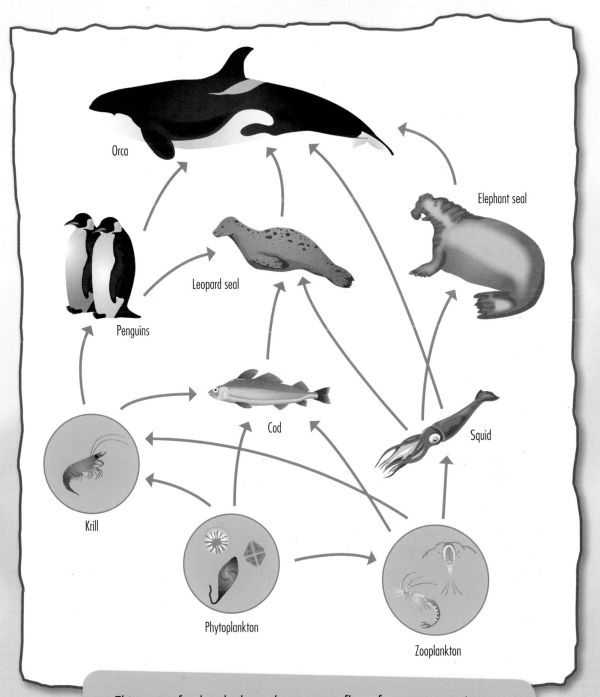

Orca

Elephant seal

Leopard seal

Penguins

Cod

Squid

Krill

Phytoplankton

Zooplankton

This ocean food web shows how energy flows from one organism to the next. Tiny, plant-like organisms called phytoplankton are at the bottom of the food web because they use sunlight to make their own food.

Hunting for food

Seals dive to find most of their food. Different species eat prey from different parts of the ocean, so some species have to dive deeper than others. Weddell seals find most of their food on the sea floor, so their dives are short but can be as deep as 600 metres (2,000 feet). Cape fur seals usually only dive to about 45 metres (150 feet) because their prey is mainly found near the surface.

The leopard seal is a powerful predator. Young leopard seals eat mainly krill but when they get older they also feed on seabirds, such as penguins, and even other smaller seals or pups. The leopard seal can catch penguins on land or in the sea. They use their powerful jaws to shake the penguin so hard that it falls apart.

HOW MUCH DO SEALS EAT?

Seals have to eat a lot of food every day because they need lots of energy for swimming and diving. For example, common seals eat 4.5 to 8.2 kilograms (10 to 18 pounds) of food a day.

Penguins make up about 87 percent of a leopard seal's diet.

Predators

Most seals are not at the top of the food chain. Predators that hunt seals include orcas, leopard seals, polar bears, and sharks. Steller sea lions have been known to feed on common seals, too. Arctic foxes and walruses eat seal pups.

Grey seals mainly eat sand eels or small fish, such as herring, but can sometimes feast on bigger fish, like this cod.

What is a seal's life cycle?

The life cycle of an animal covers its birth to its death and all the different stages in between. A seal's life cycle includes birth, youth, and adulthood. During adulthood they reproduce and have young.

Mating

At the start of the breeding season, males of some seal species **haul out** from the sea and stake out their **territory** on land. Male elephant seals can lose up to 30 per cent of their body weight during this time because they cannot leave their territory to feed. The most powerful males gather a group of females, called a harem, to mate with. Younger or weaker males have fewer opportunities to breed.

Male hooded seals will fight each other to claim land and females. They try to intimidate (scare off) each other by inflating a large hood on their head and a red balloon-like membrane from one of their nostrils.

Other male seals put on a display to attract females. This can include performing somersaults or blowing bubbles. Bearded seals and Weddell seals sing during the breeding season.

Most seals have many partners over their lifetimes but some stick with one partner for a breeding season. Crabeater seals mate on pack ice while common seals and Weddell seals mate in water.

Delayed pregnancy

Females are usually ready to mate again shortly after giving birth. However, the new baby does not start to develop inside the female straight away. Instead it takes about three months to start and then a further nine months to fully develop before the female gives birth. This ensures that the pup is born at the best time of year for it to survive.

Some seal species, such as these southern elephant seals, have a **dominant** male who can mate with as many females as he likes.

Seal pups

Fathers take no part in looking after their young. Even mothers do not stay with their young for long. Many only suckle for two to four weeks. However, the hooded seal pup is **weaned** off milk and onto normal seal food after only four days! The longest period of suckling – for the Galapagos fur seal – lasts two or three years. Mothers can only feed their pups for a short time because they cannot go into the sea to feed themselves while protecting their pups.

SPEEDY GROWTH

Pups grow quickly, gaining about 2 kilograms every day. This is because their mother's milk is 50 per cent fat. They can double their size in two weeks.

The mother of a harbour seal only stays with her pup for three to four weeks.

MOULTING

Seals moult once a year after the breeding season. Males and females moult separately. Some species lose skin as well as fur.

Seals have to come ashore to moult because they would not survive in the freezing cold water without their fur.

The cycle begins again...

Most female seals are three to six years old before they can breed. Male seals usually have to wait longer, until the age of 5 to 10. This is because of size and competition with other males. Sea lions can have young at the age of three to five. Most seals have a pup every year but some give birth every other year.

Seals are in most danger at the beginning and end of their lives. They can live for up to 30 years and sometimes longer if they can survive being a pup. Sea lions live to about the age of 20.

How do seals behave?

Seals are not usually social animals, often spending time alone. Some, such as the hooded seal, are solitary apart from during the two to three week breeding season. Not all seals are social, even when breeding. Steller sea lions, however, can be found together outside the breeding season.

Hauling out

When seals come ashore it is known as hauling out. Some species lie close together on popular beaches with little space, but others, such as the common seal, keep their distance from one another and will growl or bite if another seal gets too close. Sometimes there is a mixture of species on one beach, such as the grey and common seals that live around the UK coast.

Grey and common seals can be found together on beaches in the United Kingdom.

Icy habitat

Different species of seals haul out on beaches, rocks, or ice. Those that live on ice usually have more space. Ringed seals live in the Arctic and build **lairs** as soon as there is enough snow available. They use their claws to dig a breathing hole in the ice close to the lair and guard it carefully. There are usually several lairs and mothers move their pups between them to avoid polar bears, their main predator.

CROWDED BEACHES

With seals that breed in large groups, such as fur seals, there is a danger of pups being crushed by the huge male seals. This can happen as they rush to mate with a female, when they fight, or even when they are just moving around a crowded beach. Up to 20 per cent of pups can be killed in this way.

Polar bears mainly eat seals. When they find a seal's breathing hole, they wait for the seal to surface, and then attack.

Breathing holes

Some seals have to breathe through cracks and holes in thick ice on top of the sea, which are usually plentiful in summer. In winter, Weddell seals make and maintain breathing holes with their teeth. Over many years, a seal's teeth can wear down so much they can't eat or keep the holes open. Then the seal can die of starvation or drown under the ice.

Seals living in the polar regions, such as Weddell seals, have to make sure breathing holes are kept open.

Making noise

Seals and sea lions bark and call a lot. Males do this to warn off other males if they get too close to a female. Mothers call to find their pup when they come ashore after feeding. During the breeding season, many seal species sing to attract a mate. Both male and female leopard seals sing, but the male can sing for up to 13 hours a day!

Aggression

Seals can be aggressive. They show this by snorting, head-thrusting, and slapping the water with their flippers. Where the male of the species is much bigger than the female, males can take part in spectacular fights. They fight to control the colony and mating rights to as many females as possible.

GERALD KOOYMAN

Gerald Kooyman has investigated sea birds and sea mammals in the Antarctic for nearly 50 years. He was the first researcher to design and use a time-depth recorder to discover how deep and for how long Weddell seals dive. He found the seals dived to 700 metres (2,300 feet) for up to 82 minutes.

Male elephant seals often fight. Usually, one male will eventually back down, but sometimes fights lead to the death of one seal.

A DAY IN THE LIFE OF A SEAL

A seal's day is made up of hunting, feeding, playing, and snoozing.

FEEDING

Many seals are nocturnal, hunting and exploring at night. Crabeater seals hunt for 8 to 10 hours in a night. Hawaiian monk seals are mainly nocturnal, spending most of the day resting on the beach. This is possibly because they live in a hot place. They have as much blubber as seals living in Arctic water, so to keep cool they wallow in wet sand. Some elephant seals beat the heat in California by flipping wet sand onto their backs.

It is best not to mess with a king penguin!

PLAYING AND GROOMING

Many young seals will spend part of the day playing, often under water. The playing usually takes the form of playfighting, as practice for real fights to come. They groom themselves with their claws or sometimes by rubbing their bodies back and forth on the ground or ice.

A day in the life of a Weddell seal pup can be very tiring!

SLEEPING

Many seals rest or sleep on land. Common seals sleep at the surface of the sea in a position known as bottling. Their body is under the water with their head sticking out, allowing them to breathe more easily. It is thought that Northern elephant seals can rest or even sleep by rolling on their backs during a deep dive of up to 800 metres (2,625 feet) and sinking to the bottom of the ocean. They sink slowly by moving in circles and show no reaction when hitting the ocean floor. They then stay still for a few minutes before returning to the surface. Researchers think that sinking allows the seals to avoid near-surface predators such as orcas.

How intelligent are seals?

Intelligence is difficult to measure in animals. It usually refers to how animals hunt and maintain social relationships.

Hunting

Methods of hunting show intelligence. The Weddell seal has a clever way of diving beneath its prey and looking up. It sees the fish clearly against the light shining through cracks in the ice. Other times they blow sharply into a breathing hole. This can startle any nearby fish, making them easier to catch.

Communication

Seals use different ways of communicating in different circumstances. Males can give a very loud call when they are protecting their territory, but use a different type of call to attract females. Seals in the polar regions can make loud calls because in the vast oceans predators can not get to them so easily.

SEAL RESCUE

In 2002, a common seal saved a dog from drowning. The injured dog had fallen into the fast-flowing River Tees in Middlesbrough. It was being swept away when the seal came to its rescue. The seal circled the dog and pushed it towards the riverbank with its nose. Experts think the seal may have realized it was unusual for a dog to be in the water and so helped it onto land.

In captivity

Many of the "seals" found in zoos or marine parks are actually sea lions. Their intelligence is shown clearly by how easy they are to train in captivity. They are taught to perform tricks for the public, such as balancing a ball on their nose.

Some California sea lions have been trained to find mines and other military equipment lost under water. Some people think that training sea lions for such dangerous work is wrong.

Seals and sea lions face many threats due to human behaviour. For example, every year young harp seals in Canada are clubbed to death for their fur. Inuit people hunt some seals throughout the year, but they use all parts of the seal so that nothing is wasted.

Hunters in Canada still club to death thousands of seal pups each year.

Humans are also **polluting** oceans with industrial chemicals, litter, and oil spills. Industrial chemicals can cause serious health problems for seals. They may not be able to fight off disease or have healthy young.

Climate change

Climate change is a threat, particularly for seals living in polar regions. Rising global temperatures mean that ice is melting more rapidly and completely than before. This means less pack ice is available for seals to rest or breed on, and pups can be crushed by ice as it breaks into smaller blocks.

Fishing

The fishing industry claims that seals damage nets and eat the fish people catch. Some seals have been deliberately killed – either shot or drowned – by fishermen. There are non-harmful ways to prevent seals from eating farmed salmon, such as noise and stronger nets, but shooting them is sometimes seen as quicker and easier. In Scotland, a new law has led to a reduction in the number of seal killings, but campaigners believe that shooting should not be allowed at all. Seals can also end up as **by-catch** in the nets used to catch fish. The seals are unable to escape the nets so they drown.

When seals are caught in fishing nets, the net can cut into the seal's body, eventually leading to death.

How can people help seals?

Scientists can tag seals to learn more about where they go, how they feed, and what they eat. Some scientists use ear tags, while others use satellite transmitters attached to the seals' fur. The transmitters fall off when the seals moult, but lots of information has been gained by then. All knowledge helps when it comes to conservation.

Seal tagging helps researchers to learn about seal behaviour and how best to support them in the wild.

Conservation organizations

Conservation organizations push for governments to increase areas of marine protection to help seals and other sea mammals. A number of eared seal species, such as the Juan Fernández fur seal and the New Zealand fur seal, are now protected by law after being hunted close to **extinction**, often for their thick fur.

What you can do

Conservation organizations also try to make people more aware of the threats that sea mammals face in the wild. The more people learn and understand about seals and sea lions, the more willing they may be to help. Simple things, such as not leaving litter at the beach, can help to protect seals' habitats. You could donate some pocket money, join a conservation group, or even sponsor a seal.

SEAL RESCUES

The National Seal Sanctuary in Cornwall looks after many stranded seal pups. It costs up to £1,000 to **rehabilitate** a grey seal pup. Tagging a pup before its release allows researchers to follow the pup after it leaves the sanctuary. Tagging and following one pup costs a further £3,500.

Learn all you can about seals and the difficulties they face in the wild. Then tell your friends and family!

What does the future hold for seals?

Increases in global temperatures, overfishing, and pollution all put pressure on seals. There are many conservation groups around the world already working to protect seals and their habitats. However, more needs to be done. Efforts to further reduce pollution in our oceans have to be made. Governments need to push through updates to laws protecting seals and larger areas of ocean.

Endangered seals

While some species have huge populations, such as the 15 million crabeater seals, other species are **endangered**. It is estimated that only 1,012 Hawaiian monk seals exist and that numbers have fallen by 4.1 per cent a year since 1999.

SUCCESS STORIES

Conservation can make a huge difference. There were only a few hundred grey seals 100 years ago. However, their numbers are thought to be increasing by 7 per cent each year around the United Kingdom. On the Lincolnshire coast over 1,000 grey seals are born each year, which is up from about 12 a year just 30 years ago. The Northern elephant seal of the North Pacific is another success story. The seals were hunted for their blubber until there were fewer than 100 seals by 1910. Now, there are thought to be about 150,000 of them.

Seals are part of the ocean food chain and it is important that we don't allow them to die out. They deserve their place in the natural world. The more young people that get involved in protecting seals and sea lions, the better. Every little bit helps.

Attempts to help Hawaiian monk seals and other species are not liked by everyone. But saving these animals is important before the world loses another species.

Species profiles

Common seal

The common seal is a species of true, or earless, seal. This species profile will give you all the main facts about this fascinating sea mammal.

ears, but no ear flaps

narrow snout

fur

whiskers

back flippers

front flippers

blubber

Species: common seal, also known as harbour seal

Latin name: *Phoca vitulina*

Length: up to 1.7 metres (5.6 feet) for females; up to 1.9 metres (6.2 feet) for males

Weight: up to 130 kilograms (287 pounds) for females; up to 170 kilograms (375 pounds) for males

Habitat: coasts around the North Atlantic and North Pacific; 5 to 10 per cent of the world's population live around the United Kingdom, mainly in Scotland

Diet: fish (salmon, herring, cod), crustaceans (shrimp), and squid

Life expectancy in the wild [average]: 40 years for females; 34 years for males

Number of young: usually gives birth to one calf every year. Pregnancy lasts nine to 11 months.

New Zealand fur seal

The New Zealand fur seal is a species of eared seal. Use this species profile to find out all the main facts about this furry sea mammal.

round head

narrow snout

ears

whiskers

thick fur

front flippers

blubber

back flippers

Species: New Zealand fur seal

Latin name: *Arctocephalus forsteri*

Length: 1 to 1.5 metres (3⅓ to 5 feet) for females; up to 2.5 metres (around 8 feet) for males

Weight: 35 to 50 kilograms (77 to 110 pounds) for females; 120 to 180 kilograms (265 to 397 pounds) for males

Habitat: in the oceans around New Zealand and southern Australia, particularly the west and south of New Zealand; seen on rocky coastline during mating season

Diet: fish (mackerel, barracuda), squid, octopus

Life expectancy in the wild: up to 15 years

Number of young: usually gives birth to one calf every year. Pregnancy lasts about nine months.

Glossary

adaptation body part or behaviour of an organism that helps it survive in a particular habitat

blubber thick layer of fat on a seal's body

breed mate and produce young

by-catch fish and sea mammals caught in fishing nets that are meant to catch a different species

classification sorting of living things into groups

dominant strongest

endangered when a plant or animal is in danger of dying out

evolve change gradually over time

extinct no longer existing

food chain sequence in which one creature eats another, which eats another, and so on

food web network of intertwined food chains

gland part of the body that can produce a liquid, such as oil, that is useful to the animal in some way

groom clean the fur and skin

habitat type of place or surroundings that a living thing prefers to live in

haul out when a seal comes out of the sea onto land

hemisphere half of the world

interdependence way in which all of the living things in a habitat and the habitat itself rely on each other for survival

krill small shrimp-like creature

lair wild animal's den

mammal animal that has fur or hair, gives birth to live young, and feeds its young on milk from the mother

migrate move from one place to another, often at particular times of year

moult shed old fur and grow a new layer of fur

organism living thing

pack ice ice floating in the sea that is made by smaller pieces of ice freezing together

polar regions land and seas surrounding the North and South Poles

pollute spread harmful waste in the environment, for example in the sea

rehabilitate return to health

social living in communities or groups, in which relationships are maintained

species group of organisms that are similar and are able to produce offspring together

suckle take milk from a mother's body

tagging attaching an electronic device to an animal to study its behaviour

territory area of land that an animal views as its own

transmitter equipment attached to an animal that sends a message to a computer to allow scientists to see where the animal goes

water pressure powerful force made by water on its surroundings

wean encourage a pup to eat food other than its mother's milk

Find out more

Books

Oceans (1000 Facts), Belinda Gallagher (Miles Kelly Publishing, 2007)

Ocean Wildlife (Saving Wildlife), Sonya Newland (Franklin Watts, 2011)

Sea Hunters: Dolphins, Whales, and Seals (Wild Predators!), Andrew Solway (Heinemann Library, 2006)

Websites

www.bbc.co.uk/nature/life/Gray_Seal
Find out more about grey seals and follow the links to learn about other seals.

www.snh.org.uk/publications/on-line/naturallyscottish/seals/facts.asp
Learn some facts about seals on the Scottish National Heritage website.

Organizations to contact

International Fund for Animal Welfare
www.ifaw.org/uk
The IFAW helps to protect all animals around the world, including sea mammals.

Seals Protection Groups
www.protectourseals.org.uk
This is a group of seal protection organizations aiming to stop the shooting of seals in UK waters.

WWF UK
www.wwf.org.uk
WWF works to protect animals and nature and needs your help! Have a look at their website and see what you can do.

Index